ED. 15-

G=DOT50

Ⓝ

IN OTHER WORDS

IN
OTHER WORDS

By
FRANKLIN P. ADAMS

AUTHOR OF
"TOBOGGANING ON PARNASSUS"

GARDEN CITY   NEW YORK
DOUBLEDAY, PAGE & COMPANY
1912

To

THE W.-K. HUMAN RACE

THIS BOOK IS HOPEFULLY
DEDICATED

Craving Your Attention

Horace: Book I, Ode 32.
"Poscimur. Si quid vacui sub umbra —"

AD LYRAM

Help me, my lute, if we have ever made
  Some deathless ode, some song to live for-
    ever,
A verse to make them say: "Some serenade,
  Believe me, this her Flaccus guy is clever"—
Come, Lesbian lyre, assist me with the verses
To bring thee fame, to garner me sesterces.

Stalling his motor-boat close to the shore,
  Thine erstwhile owner smote the strings to
    Bacchus
And sang to Venus, in the midst of war,
  Be thou as kind to Mr. Q. H. Flaccus.
Dear lute, I beg, implore, invoke thee do it;
Give me thine aid, o lute! . . . Come,
  let's go to it.

CONTENTS

vii

Contents

Contents

Contents

From the Rome Herald, Nov. 29, 71 A. D.

Martial: Book IX, Epigram 81.

Though for my stuff my readers fall,
A poet likes it not at all.
But, pshaw! what time I give a feast
The cook, perhaps, is pleased the least.

IN OTHER WORDS

T. R. to W. H. T.

Or ever the knightly fight was on,
  The skirmish of smear and smudge,
I was a King in Washington
  And you were a circuit judge.

I saw, I took, I made you great,
  Friendly I called you Will,
And back in Nineteen Hundred and Eight,
  Out in Chicago, Ill.,
I made the convention nominate,
  And now — the terrible chill.

For many a sun has set and shone
  On the path we used to trudge
When I was a King in Washington
  And you were a circuit judge.

I passed the lie and you passed it back;
  You said I was all untruth;
I said that honesty was your lack;

3

In Other Words

You said I'd nor reck nor ruth.
You called me megalomaniac —
  I called you a Serpent's Tooth.

And now the convention days are gone
  And the past is full of grudge;
Yet — I was a King in Washington,
  And you were a circuit judge!

The Costofliving

This is the costofliving — $$

This is the retailer
That raises the costofliving.

This is the wholesaler
That soaks the retailer
That raises the costofliving.

This is the packer
That sticks the wholesaler
That soaks the retailer
That raises the costofliving.

This is the stockman
That charges the packer
That sticks the wholesaler
That soaks the retailer
That raises the costofliving.

This is the farmer
That stings the stockman
That charges the packer
That sticks the wholesaler
That soaks the retailer
That raises the costofliving.

In Other Words

This is the corn upon the farm
Whose cost the farmer views with alarm;
So he stings the stockman
That charges the packer
That sticks the wholesaler
That soaks the retailer
That raises the costofliving.

This is the cow with the crumpled horn,
That must be fed on the farmer's corn —
The corn the farmer grows on the farm —
The corn whose cost he views with alarm:
So he stings the stockman
That charges the packer
That sticks the wholesaler
That soaks the retailers
That raises the costofliving.

This the consumer all forlorn
Who pays for the cow with the crumpled horn —
The cow that feeds on the farmer's corn
That grows so fine on the farmer's farm —
The corn whose cost he views with alarm:
So he stings the stockman
That charges the packer
That sticks the wholesaler
That soakes the retailer
That raises the costofliving.

It's Really Disheartening

When Homer smote his you-know-what
   To sing about M. J. Ulysses,
Old Constant Reader said 'twas not
   The thing to read to youths and misses.
And Old Subscriber sent a note
   Whose words Hellenic I've forgotten —
Translated, this is what he wrote:
   "Please can this Homer simp; he's rotten."

When Q. Horatius penned a pome
   And put it in the Sabine *Journal*,
Pro Bono Publico, of Rome,
   Wrote in: "This column is infernal.
If that is humorous, good night!
   Don't tell me that you pay him money.
Whoever said this boob could write?
   Whoever told him he was funny?"

And when a column, all in rhyme,
   In solid agate, signed "John Milton,"
Appeared, some cleped him "Quince" and
      "Lime,"
   And said his stuff was very Stilton.
When Avon's bard put on a play
   Those were who said: "He can't deliver,
This William Shaxpur! Fade away!
   Good sooth, the fellow is a flivver!"

In Other Words

His path is steep, his lot is hard,
    Who Rare and Wondrous Lines composes.
Alas! to be a famous bard
    Is not an ostermoor of roses!
And if of those great poet-men
    Some folks would say: "This guy a shine
      is,"
What show have I? for now and then
    Their stuff was just as good as mine is.

More Advice

AD QUINTIUM

Horace: Book II, Ode 11.

"Quid bellicosus Cantaber et Scythes —"

O Quintius, never mind the things
    Across the Adriatic;
Let Scythian and Cantabrian kings
    Be never so emphatic,
Our board and room and clothes are paid for;
Why worry, then, what we were made for?

As I have said a thousand times,
    (Please pardon my repeating.
One has to, writing reams of rhymes.)
    The longest life is fleeting.
(Bromidic and unesoteric —
See Longfellow and Robert Herrick.)

The flowers forget the vernal green,
    The moon has many phases.
Why bother, then, the busy bean
    With the future's fogs and hazes?
Nix on the worry!   Us for Bacchus!
You, Quintius, and your Uncle Flaccus.

In Other Words

And while we're waiting for the drinks
   Here in the grotto shady,
There may appear the well-known minx,
   That lovely Lyde lady,
Who fixes up her hair so graceful —
Grab it from me, she beats an ace full.

A Bid to a House-Party

AD TORQUATUM

Horace: Book I, Epistle 5.

"Si potes Archiacis conviva recumbere lectis —"

Torquatus, if you can recline
On this cheap furniture of mine,
If you are of a mind to dare
My frugal vegetable fare,
If six-year wine may pass your throat —
Then come and visit this here pote.
My house is clean, though far from sporty;
I'll look for you about 5.40.

Some years ago to-morrow morn
Was old Augustus Cæsar born.
It is a legal holiday
And so we needn't leave the hay
Till noon.   To-night we'll fool around
Discussing light things and profound:
Girls, poetry and aviation,
And eke the future of the nation.

11

In Other Words

What use is all my coin to me
Without a friend or two or three?
The guy who's cagey with his kale
Should beat it quick to Bloomingdale.
A little wine's the proper dope,
It makes you talk and sing and hope,
Peace it promotes, for who would bicker
When plied with wine?   Hooray for licker!

The gifted author of this pome
Shall tend to everything at home;
The dishes will be clean and fine,
And how the knives and forks will shine!
Three other chaps I shall invite
(Five-handed games — are they all right?)
Nor care nor woe shall agitate us,
Come on, old scout, come on, Torquatus!

What Cut into Horace's Work

AD MAECENATEM

Horace, Epode XIV.

*"Mollis inertia cur tantam diffuderit imis
Oblivionem sensibus —"*

"What is the cause of this tardy inspiring —
  Too many juleps traversing your throat?"
Thus, my Maecenas, your ceaseless inquiring.
  Chop it, old top, it arouses my goat.

Blame not the stuff that is sacred to Bacchus;
  Cupid's the reason that pome isn't done.
He is some deity, flip it from Flaccus,
  Keeps me from finishing work I've begun.

Well, Old Anacreon had the bacillus;
  Burning affection kept him on the rack.
He couldn't work when he thought of Ba-
    thyllus
  (Read what was written on that by Anack).

As to *your* Beautiful Lady, Maecenas,
  Helen herself was no fairer a frail.
Phryne the flirt, but consid'able Venus,
  Keeps *me* from work for THE EVENING
    MAIL.

13

Horace on Contentment

Book II, Ode 18.

"Non ebur neque aureum
Mea renidet in domo lacunar —"

Within my modest home nor ivory gleams,
  Nor in my room a golden ceiling glitters;
No pillars mine from Africa's extremes,
  No purple spun by lovely lady-knitters.
I'm poor but honest, and — you'll give me
    credit —
Some poet, too. Some poet's right; you said
    it.

For further favors I do not implore
  The gods above nor any human being;
My Sabine farm's enough. I ask no more.
  I never argue with the fates' decreeing.
Day follows day. I never dared to doubt it.
Suppose I did? What could I do about it?

And yet the very marble newly hewn,
  The very stone you gaze at, eager, merry,
That stone may lie above you very soon
  In Forest Hills, the well-known ceme-tery.
And still, instead of charity and penance,
You raise the rent and disposses your tenants.

14

Horace on Contentment

But stay!   Despite your wondrous wealth and
 fame,
 None is so sure as Plato, so rapacious —
You cannot beat, you cannot tie his game;
 The grave that yawns for rich and poor is
 spacious.
(TRANSLATOR'S NOTE: Q. H. was euphemistic.
They used to say.   *I* call him socialistic.)

"Simplicity"

AD PUERUM

Horace: Book I, Ode 38.

"Persicos odi, puer apparatus —"

The Persian pomp and circumstance are
    things I do not like;
I shall not buy a motor-car while I possess a
    bike;
I will not buy a Panama to place upon my
    head,
A simple sennitt bonnet, boy, purchase for
    me instead.

For such a thatch will do for you as it has
    done for me —
An ordinary straw hat, for a dollar thirty-
    three.
Then to the coolest bar in town for some
    Milwaukee liquor
Where I may watch the ball-game — as it
    comes over the ticker.

Getting Lydia's Number

AD LYDIAM

Horace: Book I, Ode 8.

"Lydia, dic, per omnis —"

Lydia, by the gods above,
  Tell me why, O maid magnetic,
You must ruin with your love
  Him that used to be athletic?

Tell me why, O maid magnetic,
  Sybaris will not cavort —
Him that used to be athletic,
  Him that used to be a sport?

Sybaris will not cavort
  On the field or in the river —
Him that used to be a sport
  With the quoit or with the quiver!

On the field or in the river,
  On the court or on the links,
With the quoit or with the quiver —
  You're his Jonah, you're his Jinx!

On the court or on the links
  Sybaris was once a wonder,
You're his Jonah, you're his Jinx —
  Why delight to drag him under?

In Other Words

Sybaris was once a wonder
  You must ruin with your love.
Why delight to drag him under?
  Lydia, by the gods above!

Spring Pome

AD SEXTIUM

Horace: Book II, Ode 4.

"Solvitur acris hiems grata —"

The backbone of winter is shattered to pieces;
    The breezes are balmy that blow from the
        west;
The farmer his cows from the stable releases;
    The ploughman gets up from his fireside
        domest;
No more are the meadows all icy and snowy;
    Come columns on Mathewson, Sweeney and
        Kling;
The strawberry shortcake is heavy and
    doughy —
                'Tis Spring!

Now Venus, the w. k. Cytherean,
    Cavorts Isadorably under the moon,
Assisted by choruses gracile, nymphean,
    She dances a measure that's wholly jejune.
'Tis time to divert one's estraying attention
    To bonnets embowered with every old
        thing —
Fruits, myrtle and parsley — again I must
    mention
                'Tis Spring!

19

In Other Words

'Tis time for the sacrifice sacred to Faunus —
   He may get our lambkin, he may get our
      goat.
O Sextius, ere death shall have wholly with-
      drawn us,
   Take this from Horatius, your favorite pote;
Soon Pluto will call you, at some unforeseen
      time,
   You'll go, be you journalist-jester or king,
You can't get away from it. But, in the
      meantime,
        'Tis Spring!

A Sealed Proposal

AD CHLOËN

Horace: Book I, Ode 23.

"Vitas hinnuleo me similis, Chloë —"

Nay, Chloë, dear, forget your fear,
   Nor like a frightened fawn outrun me;
No savage I to horrify —
        You shouldn't shun me.

Come, Chloë, queen, you're seventeen;
   There's many a precedent to back us.
Why shouldn't you be Mrs. Q.
        Horatius Flaccus?

Cheer Up, Postumus

AD POSTUMUM

Horace, Book II, Ode 14.

"Eheu! fugaces,   Postume,   Postume —"

O Postumus, dear Postumus, Old Father
    Time's a sprinter,
The summer of my life is spent, approaches
    now the winter;
Nor all my Wit nor Piety, to quote Omar Fitz-
    gerald,
Can keep my obit from appearing in the Sabine
    Herald.

If for a daily sacrifice you killed three hundred
    cattle,
Think you that it would keep from you the
    Dread and Final Rattle?
Nix! Though you build eight colleges and
    lib'ries eighty-seven,
You can't avoid what Rhyme demands I
    designate as Heaven.

Cheer Up, Postumus

Your home, your wife, your family, your
    uncles, ay! and your aunts —
You'll have to leave 'em all behind. (Have
    you enough insurance?)
And O, the cobwebbed Caecuban now aging
    in your cellar
You'll have to deed to some one who's a nice,
    deserving feller.

The Good Old Socialistic Days

IN SUI SAECULI LUXURIAM

Horace: Book II, Ode 15.

"Jam pauca aratro jugera regiae —"

With skyscrapers building a dozen a day,
   I am anxious, I View-with-Alarm;
And I'd like to know how there'll be room for
     the plow,
   And what's going to become of the farm.

Time was when the olive was w. k.,
   Now myrtle and violet are in.
I urge on this nation of Rome, Conservation —
   This waste is a shame and a sin.

When Romulus reigned and when Cato was
     king,
   Conditions were never so tough;
The Morgans and such hadn't any too much,
   And the poorest had more than enough.

Return once again, O ye days that I sing,
   When Labor was wearing a crown!
O life was more spacious, grab this from
     Horatius,
   When Rome was a Socialist town.

24

A Plea for the Present

AD LEUCONOEM.

Horace: Book I, Ode 11.

"Tu ne quaesieris, scire nefas —"

Be not, I pray, so curious
For knowledge; it's injurious
      To know about the future
      And compute your
         Every chance.
'Twould be a source of pain to you
To find what years remain to you
      To know your length of tether
      And the weather
         In advance.

Life? Don't have such a thirst of it;
The best you get's the worst of it!
      You can't be here forever,
      They assever.
         Watch your step!
While I've been oratorical
Pa Tempus (metaphorical)
      Has, as it were, been guying
      Me by flying.
         — Are you hep?

Indorsing Xanthias's Choice

AD XANTHIUM PHOCEUM.

Horace: Book II, Ode 4.

"Ne sit ancillae tibi amor pudori,
Xanthia Phoceu!"

Don't let your yearning for your cook,
    O Xanth, give you the willies.
Remember how Brisëis, though a slave,
    aroused Achilles;
The Telamonian Ajax young Tecmessa made a
    hit with;
And Agamemnon had a maid whom he was
    awful smit with.
Why, I would give you 8 to 5 — and I am far
    from gambly —
That Phyllis is descended from some fine old
    Southern fam'ly.
Accept it from the occupant of this here con-
    ning steeple:
As nice a girl as she is must have come from
    Lovely People.
Look at her arms — they're perfect! So the
    beauty of her face is;
And — as an artist — I indorse her — well,
    her other graces.
Nay, be not jealous of the bard, my Xanthias!
    Remember
Your uncle will be forty-one the seventh of
    September.

Horace to Maecenas

THE BARD ASKED HIS PATRON FOR BASEBALL TICKETS

Maecenas, in many an ode
  I've jollied and flattered and praised you,
    In metre Glyconic, alcaic, adonic,
      I've mentioned you dozens of times.
The virtues that I have bestowed
  On you! and the heights where I've raised
    you!
      You pander and pet me, but what does
      it get me?
      I want some reward for my rhymes.

I've called you a great little guy
  Right n. p. r. m., top o' colyum;
    I've pinned some verbenas on you, Bill
    Maecenas,
    And all that I got was a drink —
A pint of Old Caecuban Rye!
  My verses to you'd fill a volume.
    You used to command me, but now,
    y'understand me,
    I've quit being Marcus O'Gink.

In Other Words

Maecenas, you get me, I hope.
   I want a reply to my queries;
      They're plain and vocalic, in 8-point
        italic,
      And clear as a midsummer sky
This, then, is the drift of my dope:
    Do I get a seat for The Series?
    Am I to be present next Sat. if it's
      pleasant?
    Maecenas, I pause for reply.

"Good-by, My Lover, Good-by!"

AD PYRRHAM

Horace: Book I, Ode 5.

"Quis multa gracilis te puer in rosa —"

O pretty Pyrrha, false as fair,
For whom dost thou do up thy hair,
Thy crown of gold, thy shining tresses?
What gracile youth gives thee caresses?

Alas!   How often shall he find
The faithlessness of womankind!
As who should say, in utter wonder,
"How fair it was!   Who thought of thunder?"

Ah — wretched they that think thee fair,
Enmeshed in thy seductive snare!
I vow, by Neptune, ne'er to woo thee
Again, for I am jerry to thee.

Thoughts on Matters and Things

AD GROSPHUM

Horace: Book II, Ode 16.
"Otium divos rogat impotenti
Pressus Ægæo —"

Grosphus, a guy who's sailing in a tempest
On the Aegean when the moon is hidden —
He wants a rest, while stewing in his state-
room,
    Weary and seasick.

Weary of war, what do the Thracians yearn
for?
What seek the Medes, with quivers full of
arrows?
What can't you buy with purple, gold or
rubies?
    Rest is the answer.

Not Morgan's cash, nor Rockefeller's money,
No blue-and-brass can drive away the willies
Caused by the care of elegant apartments,
    Rugs and swell ceilings.

Thoughts on Matters and Things

Wise the gazabe upon whose simple table
Old-fashioned truck like salt-and-pepper
    castors
Yet may be found. His bean is never both-
    ered —
    Sleeps like a hallboy.

Why do we fuss for one thing and another?
Why do we hike to Saranac or Newport?
How can a human leave himself behind him?
    Answer: He cannot.

Worry can get a guy on the Olympic;
Worry can chase a colonel in the Army;
Swift as the wind, to use a new expression —
    Care is some sprinter.

Merry and bright, the citizen who's cheerful
Won't worry much about to-morrow's break-
    fast.
"No one," he smiles, "who faces Time the
    pitcher
    Wallops one thousand."

There was Achilles, cut off in his twenties,
And, *au contraire*, Tithonus was a hundred:
I may be lucky; you might be run over
    Most any morning.

In Other Words

You've got a farm with fancy sheep and
     heifers;
You've got a mare all curry-combed and
     glossy;
Purple silk socks and purple fancy weskits —
     You're a swell dresser.

And what has Fate, the undeceitful, slipped
     me?
Only a small apartment out in Harlem,
And, with a trick of turning snappy Sapphics,
     Scorn for the roughnecks.

On an Upright Life

AD ARISTIUM FUSCUM

Horace: Book I, Ode 22.

[Those whom the original verbiage may confuse are advised to read only the italics: those who detest our efforts may read only Q. H. Flaccus's words, set of course in Roman; and the rest may combine them.]

(Integer vitae) *A man who's on the level,*
  (Non eget . . . arcu) *He needn't have a*
    fear;
(Nec venenatis) *Not arrows of the devil*
  (Fusce, pharetra) *Can harm a conscience*
    clear —

(Sive per Syrtes) *Whether he's in Peoria,*
  (Sive facturus) *New York or Newtonville,*
(Caucasum vel) *East Orange or Emporia,*
  (Lambit Hydaspes) *Or Pocahontas, Ill.*

(Namque me . . . lupus) *For once, when*
    I was singing,
  (Dum meam . . . Lalagen) *A wolf*
    came up to me;
(Terminum curis) *He heard my lyric ringing,*
  (Fugit inermem) *And fled immejitlee.*

In Other Words

(Quale portentum.) *Believe me, he was some
     wolf,*
  (Daunias latis) *Not wood from Noah's Ark,*
(Nec Jubae tellus) *No little Daunian bum wolf*
  (Arida nutrix) *Like those in Central Park.*

(Pone me, pigris) *O put me on the prairie,*
  (Arbor aestiva) *Or let me hire a hall,*
Quod latus mundi) *Set me upon Mt. Airy,*
  (Jupiter urget) *Or anywhere at all.*

(Pone sub curru) *Still I, on the equator,*
  (Solis . . . negata) *At ninety in the
     shade,*
(Dulce ridentem) *Shall love — a poor trans-
     lator —*
  (Dulce loquentem) *My sweetly smiling
     maid.*

The Stinging of V. Catullus, Esq.

(Which is his 70th Ode, dry-cleaned and rekalsomined)

Myrtilla says that there is none
   So strong, so fine, so cavalierly,
From New Rochelle to Evanston,
         As yours sincerely.

She says that no one else is half
   So utterly attractive to her,
That she'd give Jove himself the laugh
         If he should woo her.

I say she SAYS so . . . Ah, I find
   The words of Eve's most lovely daughter
Ought to be written on the wind
         In running water!

V. Catullus Said in Part:

(Being a shy at the Fifty-first Ode.)

Whose seat is opposite to thine,
My Lesbia, seems to me divine;
For it were heaven to be so near thee,
To gaze upon thee and to hear thee.

But, lowlife lyrist that I am,
I see thee, and am like a clam;
My tongue is mute; my heart's a lead one;
Sight, hearing fail me — I'm a dead one!

The Mathematics of Catullus

Ode 7.

"Quaeris quot mihi basiationes
Tuae, Lesbia, sint satis, superque?"

Lesbia, you would have me state
  What the number is
Of the times to osculate.
Let your pote approximate,
  Namely, t'wit, and viz:

Lesbia, count the sands that lie
  On the spicy shore;
Sum the stars that in the sky
Coruscate; and multiply
  That by thousands more —

That, O sweetest of your sex,
  Fails the full amount.
Let the total number vex
All the jealous rubbernex
  Trying to keep count!

Catullus to His Knockers

AD AURELIUM ET FURIUM

Ode 16.

If now and then I spill a pome
  That seems too peppery for a paper
Subscribers take into The Home —
  Too filled with chili sauce and caper —
Because I'm fresh and will not shut up
You think that I'm an awful cut-up.

A poet in the major league
  Must lead a life above suspicion,
Though he may write of love, intrigue,
  Society and prohibition.
His stuff has got to be so snappy
That it will make all ages happy.

Cease, lowlifes, then, to lamp my line;
  Your knocking never shall upset me.
I lyricize of love and wine,
  And those who care for such will get me.
And you who don't — oh, yes, I mean you,
Aurelius, Furius — I'll bean you!

Handing It to Cynthia

Propertius: Book II, Elegy 5.

"Hoc verumst, tota te ferri Cynthia Roma
Et non ignota vivere nequitia?"

O Cynthia, tell me, is it true
  That you're not acting fit to print?
That Roman clubdom talks of you
  And whispers things I may not hint?
What has this gossip of the street meant?
Do I deserve that sort of treatment?

Tush! I shall seek some other skirt
  Who loves to lamp her printed name
In poems written by Propert.
  Me for a grateful kind of dame.
Before you get a chance to con me,
I'll do it — while the peeve is on me.

For lovers' quarrels disappear
  As clouds before the southern wind,
Wherefore I say, let's cut it here,
  Before we knot the ties that bind.
You'll weep and wail and sob and sorrow,
But you'll forget it all to-morrow.

39

In Other Words

I shall not biff you with a brick
   Nor pull your hair.   I scorn to spleen.
I leave such actions to the hick
   Who wears no laurel on his bean.
Far subtler you shall find my curses;
Your cheek shall pale at these here verses!

The Beefing of S. Propertius, Esq.

AD TULLUM

Book I, Elegy 1.

"Cynthia prima suis miserum me cepitocellis —"

Cynthia first and the wonderful eyes of her
   Taught me the meaning of Love and
      Romance;
Now I have sung to the stars and the skies of
      her —
   Love has diluted the pride of my glance.

Ah! 'tis a year, yet the madness diminishes
   Never a fraction, a tittle, or jot,
Though I anticipate well what the finish is,
   Though I bewail my unfortunate lot.

Tullus, Milanion traveled the universe
   Till Atalanta was thrall to his heart,
Futile my pleading and vain is my tuny verse,
   Zero's the sum of my amorous art.

Witches that lure by some sorcery-ritual
   Luna right down from the regular sky,
I shall concede that your power is habitual
   An ye make Cynthia paler than I!

In Other Words

And, O my friends who have warned me too
    tardily,
  Let me but utter the truth in my mind,
I'll endure iron and suffer foolhardily . . .
  Luck, wedded friends I am leaving behind!

No luck for me . . . Here is counsel
    gratuitous:
  Cleave to your true love forever plus aye;
Else, if your path be a trifle circuitous,
  How you'll remember my words of to-day!

Indorsing a w. k. Emotion

AD TULLUM

Propertius: Book I, Elegy 14.

"Tu licet abjectus Tibernia molliter unda—"

Though by the Tiber you recline,
Luxurious, inert, supine,
Drinking five quarts of Lesbian wine,
   Or six.
I'm in the know, grab this from me:
That, and the wealth of Old Johndee
Plus seven multiplied by three,
   Is nix.

Nope. Me for Love. When I'm with Cynth,
I, modest writer of this Plinth,
Am jutht ath good ath any printh;
   And, say,
If she should suddenly grow cold,
What then would help Pierp Morgan's gold?
By millions could I be cajoled?
   Nay, nay!

Propertius Confesses

AD DEMIPHONEM

Book II, Elegy 18.

"Scis here mi multas pariter placuisse puellas.
Scis mihi, Demophoön —"

You know, my Dem, that each P. M. I comb the
    gay Rialto
  (Posterity will say I was a James Buchanan
    Brady,
And any frail can have my kale, soprano or
    contralto —
  You're c. to k. the reason why my theme is
    only Lady.

Tush: ask a guy the reason why the days are
    short in winter,
  And ask him why is water wet and why's a
    ballet dancer,
And where's the snow of long ago, or ask why
    is a printer —
  Old top, it's just my temp'rament. There
    ain't no other answer.

Roman Innuendo

Martial: Book I, Epigram 72.

O Fidentinus, when you steal —
   My words are chosen and impartial —
My stuff, it is a phony deal
   You put across on M. V. Martial.

Thus Aegle thinks the teeth she wears,
   So sozodontalish and pearly,
Are hers; thus black Lycoris swears,
   Daubed with white lead, she is Some Girlie.

Bard of the Mrs. Harris school,
   (This stanza should be double-leaded),
As you're a poet now, so you'll
   Have lots of hair when you're bald-headed!

To Julia, on June 21

[In the Elizabethan manner.]

Thou askest of me why to-day,
   My Julia, I do love thee moe;
And thou art fain to have mee saie
   Wherefore I am affected soe.

An thou wouldst wit the reasoun of
   Thyself to-day beeing more dere
Than othertime, it is, my love,
   The longest day of all the yere.

Martial's Bit of a Joke

Epigrams II, 38.

Linus, you are c2k
What I grow from day to day
At my Sabine spot suburban.
Pipe — and paste it in your turban:

Try it on your piccolo,
Linus: this is what I grow:
(Get my snappy repartee, you)
Happy that I do not see you.

A Ballade of Known and Unknown Matters

BY FRANCOIS VILLON

[EDITOR'S NOTE: One of the things we know less than we do others is how to translate French. And so, to translate another of Mons. Villon's refrains, "We cry you mercy, every one."]

I'm not a simp; I'm not a joe;
　I'm on when cream is full of flies.
By what they wear I always know
　A lot about these dressy guys.
　I know the black from sunny skies;
I know a staller from a pep;
　I know the phony from the prize —
But to myself I am not hep.

I'm jerry to the fashions, bo;
　I cop the clerics by their ties;
I know the chieftain from Poor Lo,
　And cherry tarts from blueb'ry pies.
　I know the con men and the Cys;
I know "Both gates!" and "Watch your
　　　step!";
　I know the Bourbons from the ryes —
But to myself I am not hep.

48

A Ballade of Matters

A dray is not a tally-ho;
  (That is a thing I realize).
I know 16 from Double-O,
  Ben Davises from Northern Spies.
  I know some frails who have some eyes;
I know the honey from the skep;
  I know just how to balladize,
But to myself I am not hep.

L'ENVOI.

Prince, I am Jeremiah Wise,
  Clutch it from me, that is my **rep**:
Excepting only this revise:
  But to myself I am not hep.

The Translated Way

I

" Wenn ich in deine Augen seh',
So schwindet all mein Leid und weh "

When I into your eyes do see
So goes away my woe from me,
And, too, when I your mouth do kiss
So gains my health a benefice.

When I upon your bosom lie
It comes o'er me like joy from sky,
And when you speak it: "I love thee!"
So must I weep quite bitterly.

II

"Ich hab' im Traum geweinet."

I have in a dream been weeping,
    Medreamt thou didst lie underground,
Then wakened I up and the tears flowed
    Still down from my cheek all around.

I have in a dream been weeping,
    Medreamt thou didst me forget,
Then wakened I up, I continued
    Crying long, bitterly yet.

The Translated Way

I have in a dream been weeping,
   Medreamt thou wert to me yet good,
Then wakened I up and still always
   My tears did come down in flood.

III

"Hör ich das Liedchen klingen,
Das einst die Liebste sang,"

Hear I the songlet singing
   That once the dearest sang,
From out my breast upspringing
   There comes wild painful pang.

Impels me one dark languish
   That high wood to attain,
Dissolves in teardrops' anguish
   My extraordinary pain.

IV

"Was will die einsame Thraene?"

What wants the teardrop single?
   She mists my glance with pains.
She back from olden times yet
   Within mine eye remains.

She had many glittering sisters
   Who all have taken flight,
With my torments and my gladnesses
   Dissolved they in wind and night.

Like clouds have disappeared, also,
   The diminutive stars so blue
That in every torment and gladness
   My heart would smile into.

In Other Words

Oh, likewise my love has vanished
　Like to a trifling sigh,
Though old, individual teardrop,
　Now too, disappear, pray I!

The Height of Disagreeableness

A window rattling in the night
   When I am fain for sleep
Gives me, I own, a sort of fright,
   And makes my flesh to creep.

A discord jars my very soul;
   A peach-skin makes me feel
As low within the depths of dole
   As a dentist's emery wheel.

The brakes upon a Broadway car;
   A cat; a crying child;
The filing of a saw — these are
   Some things that drive me wild.

But of all creepy things accursed,
   Of various kinds and brands,
I hold this as the very worst:
   A barber with cold hands.

As to Eyes

Lady, better bards than I,
  Poets of an elder day,
Seemed to love to versify
  On "her eyes," or blue or gray.

'T is an oft-recurrent theme
  For the bards who rhapsodize;
Not a one but used to dream
  Of the loveliness of eyes.

Shelley, Tennyson and Keats,
  Swinburne, Byron, Moore and Burns —
All had visual conceits,
  All had various optic yearns.

Far from me to mimimize
  Elder, better bards, except
This: they spoke of lady's eyes
  Haunting them what time they slept.

Envy I those troubadours.
  I am such a helpless thrall,
Lady, when I think of yours,
  I — I cannot sleep at all.

The Truth About the Spratts

As to the meat that was upon
   The J. Spratts' bill-of-fare —
Now, Mrs. Spratt liked hers well done
   While Jack preferred his rare.

Jack Spratt liked lots of light,
   His wife desired it dim,
For her the shaded lamp and low —
   The 32s for him.

Jack Spratt liked lots of air,
   All windows opened wide,
While Mrs. S. detested draughts —
   "This flat is cold!" she cried.

Jack Spratt liked comedies.
   The missus liked to weep
At dismal dramas, such as put
   Her lawful spouse to sleep.

John Spratt, he hated bridge;
   His consort was a fiend.
Who always would suggest a game
   Whenever friends convened.

In Other Words

J. Spratt liked keeping house,
   His wife preferred to board.
"Nothing like that for Colonel Spratt!"
   Declared her liegest lord.

Jack Spratt was all for prose,
   His wife was all for rhyme;
And so betwixt them both, you see,
   They had a helova time.

Campaign Thoughts

This is a presidentiai year.
   (An unassailable reflection.)
"Things will be better," so we hear,
      "After election."

Now comes the questing of the Vote,
   The Call to Arms, the Appeal to Reason,
The Keynote Speech, the Clarion Note —
      This is the season

When everywhere and roundabout,
   From coast to coast, and vicy-versy,
The candidates will speak and spout,
      Sans fear or mercy;

When from the Peerless Pines of Maine
   To California's Pebbly Beaches,
We are enthralled by the campaign,
      And many speeches.

Perhaps I ought to add "enthralled,"
   (Cf. line 3, above tetrastich)
As Mr. Ward once might have drawled
      Was wrote sarkastick.

In Other Words

And therefore I demand a word,
    A message to This Glorious Nation.
I crave the right of being heard
        On Conservation.

On Conservation: Not of trees
    Of waterways, or fish, or horses —
Of something greater far than these:
        Human Resources

Resources wasted in campaigns,
    In oratory dry and juiceless.
The waste of energy and brains
        Strikes me as useless.

For him I'd vote who said "Enough!
    I scorn the terrible traditions
Of the campaign.   I leave that stuff
        To politicians."

That's all.   I might do five or six
    More stanzas, but I find it dreary.
Do you care much for politics?
        They make *me* weary.

Everybody's Overdoing It

[Provoked by having heard, in a single week, "That
Beautiful Tune," "Alexander's Ragtime Band," "That
Swaying Harmony," "Banjo Tunes," "That Mesmer-
izing Mendelssohn Tune," "Play Dat Barbershop
Chord," "Rum Tum Tiddle," "Pick, Pick, Pick on the
Mandolin," "That Haunting Melody," "That Coon-
town Quartette," "I Love to Hear an Irish Band Play
on St. Patrick's Day," "That Slippery Slide Trom-
bone," "The Ragtime Violin," "That Mysterious
Rag," "Mello-Cello Melody," "That Raggedy Rag,"
"That Chicken Glide," "That Dramatic Rag," "That
Italian Serenade" and "Brass Band Ephraim Jones."]

Whenever I go to a vo-da-vil show —
    A thing that I frequently do —
The stunts that I see which are pleasing to me
    Are painfully, fearfully few.
The acrobats eight are an act that I hate;
    The monkeys and dogs I detest.
And the comedy kind that are known as re-
    fined
    Are as dull as an almanac jest.
But of all the sad things that variety brings
    The worst of the wearisome throng
Is the fury and craze of these "musical" days:
    The song that entreats for a song.

In Other Words

And when some one begins to demand violins,
    Or "That Sinewy So-and-So Strain,"
I want to get out, and, departing, to shout
    The following earnest refrain:

CHORUS

Cut out asking for that ragtime song
    As played by that melodious coon!
Cease to bellow for that syncopated 'cello!
    Quit teasing for that tremulous tune!
Stop that yearning for that raggedy rag!
    Stop asking for that glidey guff!
Cut out this thing of begging folks to sing,
    And cut out the "Please-Play" stuff!

I've heard them demand a harmonica band;
    I've heard people crave a cornet;
And even "Play some on that old kettle-
      drum!"
    Or "Fillip that flageolet!"
I've heard singers long for that "Love's Old
      Sweet Song,"
    And yell for "That Old Time Quadrille";
I've heard 'em insist on Puccini and Liszt,
    And yearn for that Trovatore trill;
They ask for Bellini, Balfe, Wagner, Rossini,
    The while, in unscrupulous zeal.
The people who "write" a new song in a night
    Grow rich on the tunes that they steal.

Everybody's Overdoing It

And that's why I moan in this querulous tone,
  And that's what is deep in my heart;
And if one should beseech me to offer a speech,
  I'd do it, responding, in part:

CHORUS.

Cut out asking for that "Magic Flute,"
  And that "Tannhäuser" overture!
Cease to yell for that "William Tell,"
  And "The Bride of Lammermoor!"
Stop that music-hunger all around,
  Plenty is quite Enough.
Stop your praying for incessant playing,
  And cut out the "Please-Sing" stuff!

Baseball's Sad Lexicon

These are the saddest of possible words:
  "Tinker to Evers to Chance."
Trio of bear cubs, and fleeter than birds,
  Tinker and Evers and Chance.
Ruthlessly pricking our gonfalon bubble,
Making a Giant hit into a double —
Words that are heavy with nothing but
        trouble:
  "Tinker to Evers to Chance."

To Myrtilla, on Opening Day

Myrtilla, ere the season starts,
  Or e'er the primal ball be thrown
If you would win this callous heart's
  Affection for your very own,
This counsel, blooming, fresh and frondent —
Accept it from your correspondent.

Back in the days of Old Cap Anse
  'Twas reckoned cute to spoof a dame,
And famed was her incognitance
  About the so-called national game;
And comment feminine was silly.
That was before your day, Myrtilly.

For, now, Myrtilla, I admit
  Your knowledge far transcends mine own;
You know an error from a hit —
  A quaver from a semitone;
You never say "How small the bat is!"
You never have to ask who that is.

Nay, Myrt, too well you like the game;
  You are too true a devotee;
My Blue-Print is the kind of dame
  Whose love is less for ball than me;
And so, my Myrt, that is the reason
I think I'll go alone this season.

A Ballplayer's Day

"Sweet are the uses of advertisement."

OLD SONG

The famous pitcher woke at eight
   To one of GUFF'S ALARUM CLOCKS,
Put on a suit of AERO-GREAT,
   And donned a pair of SILKO-SOX.

Then, lathered well with SMEAREM'S SOAP,
   He shaved with BOREM'S RUSTLESS
      BLADE;
Did on a suit of heliotrope —
   THE KAMPUS KUT in every shade.

Then berries served with JORDAN'S CREAM
   And eggs from BUNKEM'S DAIRY
      FARM;
Then, as he read THE MORNING SCREAM,
   He smoked a pipe of LUCKY CHARM.

Then, donning one of BEANEM'S HATS,
   He rode out in his WHATSTHECAR;
Played ball; then home to RENTEM'S
      FLATS
   To smoke a SHUTEMOUT CIGAR.

A Ballplayer's Day

He listened to his WAXAPHONE,
　　Then lay — ending his day so rough —
Upon a mattress widely known.
　　*　　　*　　　*　　　*　　　*

　　But, at the price, I've said enough.

Ever See Her?

There was a little fluff,
And she wore a little puff
　　And a rat made of shoddy and of cotton.
When they were there
She looked very, very fair,
　　And when they were off she looked rotten.

A Ballad of Baseball Burdens

The burden of hard hitting.   Slug away
  Like Honus Wagner or like Tyrus Cobb.
Else fandom shouteth: "Who said you could
    play?
  Back to the jasper league, you minor slob!"
  Swat, hit, connect, line out, get on the job.
Else you shall feel the brunt of fandom's ire
  Biff, bang it, clout it, hit it on the knob —
This is the end of every fan's desire.

The burden of good pitching.   Curved or
    straight.
  Or in or out, or haply up or down,
To puzzle him that standeth by the plate,
  To lessen, so to speak, his bat-renown:
  Like Christy Mathewson or Miner Brown,
So pitch that every man can but admire
  And offer you the freedom of the town —
This is the end of every fan's desire.

A Ballad of Baseball Burdens

The burden of loud cheering. O the sounds!
  The tumult and the shouting from the
    throats
Of forty thousand at the Polo Grounds
  Sitting, ay, standing *sans* their hats and
    coats.
  A mighty cheer that possibly denotes
That Cub or Pirate fat is in the fire;
  Or, as H. James would say, We've got their
    goats —
This is the end of every fan's desire.

The burden of a pennant. O the hope,
  The tenuous hope, the hope that's half a
    fear,
The lengthy season and the boundless dope,
  And the bromidic; "Wait until next year."
  O dread disgrace of trailing in the rear,
O Piece of Bunting, flying high and higher
  That next October it shall flutter here:
This is the end of every fan's desire.

ENVOY

Ah, Fans, let not the Quarry but the Chase
  Be that to which most fondly we aspire!
For us not Stake, but Game; not Goal, but
    Race —
  THIS is the end of every fan's desire.

John Jones, Clerk

John Jones, he was a faithful clerk
  As any now alive;
You'd always find him at his work
  From eight o'clock till five.

Without a single minute's loss
  He worked the tedious days,
Till once he said: "I'll strike the boss
  For just a little raise."

"Why, Jones," replied the Leader then,
  "How can you be so base?
Why, I could get a hundred men
  To-day to take your place."

So Jones apologized, and turned
  Back to his daily books,
Until his nature fairly yearned
  For fields and trees and brooks.

"I need a rest," requested Jones,
  "Please, sir, may I be spared?"
Whereat the Boss in honeyed tones
  Accordingly declared:

John Jones, Clerk

"Why, John, old chap, I'd like to let
  You off for half a year;
But how would this old business get
  Along without you here?"

One More

Another difference, meseems,
  Betwixt the twain, forsooth;
The optimist has illusions,
  The pessimist knows the truth.

"And the Only Tune that He Could Play"

Jane, Jane, my upstairs neighbor,
Learned to play with lots of labor,
But the only thing she ever would play
Was the sextet from "Lu-ci-a."

Tom, Tom, the man below,
Plays for hours on the pi-an-o,
Plays no tune but the "Melody in F,"
And only that in the treble clef.

Across the court is a Fair Unknown
Who loves to listen to the Talkiphone,
And the only record she cares to spring
Is that "Every Little Movement" thing.

Mary, Mary, quite contrary,
Loves to practise the "Miserere";
Ben, Ben, the gink next door us,
Knows no tune but "The Pilgrims' Chorus."

Thorns, Rifts, Clouds, Flaws, Blemishes, Etc.

["The attitude of mind I have always believed in, is to answer, when anybody says how ugly Mrs. Blank's nose is, 'Yes, but hasn't she a lovely complexion?'" — KATE DOUGLAS WIGGIN.]

Would I were constructed so!
   Would I failed to find the flaws!
But when people talk of Poe
   With consid'able applause
I concede that he was There;
   That his name is deep engraven
On the scroll; "But," I declare,
   "I can't see much in 'The Raven.'"

People prate of Dryden's dope,
   But his rhymes were often false;
There are some good things in Pope,
   But his meter often halts.
Take the things that Wordsworth wrote,
   Some — I hate to hurl the hammer —
Are not worthy of a pote;
   Shelley made some slips in grammar.

In Other Words

Horace Greeley wrote a fist
   That a comp. could never read;
Byron — yes, if you insist,
   He could write, I will concede —
But his private history
   Was a riot and a panic —
Inexcusable by me,
   Stern, unbending, Puritanic.

Would I sensed a Thornless Rose!
   Would I heard a Riftless Lute!
Would, despite that lady's nose,
   I could say "But she's a beaut."
Would that I might ever see
   But the True, the Fair, the Youthful!
Would — oh, would that I might be
   Optimistic — and untruthful!

"May Recover"

There was a man in our town,
    And he was wondrous hot;
He jumped into a Broadway bar
    For the contents of a bot.

And when he found it made him warm
    To drink of Scotch or rye,
He jumped into another bar
    Another drink to buy.

As John Howard Payne said—

There's a popular impression tantamount to
     an obsession,
  We have read of it in article and pome,
That vacationers returning undergo a lot of
     yearning
        To be home.

We have seen a lot of verses on the emptiness
     of purses
  Caused by going to the mountain or the
     shore,
How the dolce far niente thing is often more
     than plenty,
        And a bore.

Wheeze and whimsy, fact and fable on the
     poorness of the table,
  Gag and giggle on the hardness of the bed —
Of the myriad deprivations to the goers on
     vacations
        We have read.

As to all that sort of patter touching on va-
     cation matter,
  We arise in modest wise to interject
That the folks who knock the rural thing —
     or things, to make it plural —
        Are correct.

For the Other 364 Days

Christmas is over. Uncork your ambition!
Back to the battle! Come on, competition!
Down with all sentiment, can scrupulosity!
Commerce has nothing to gain by jocosity;
Money is all that is worth all your labors;
Crowd your competitors, nix on your neigh-
      bors!
Push 'em aside in a passionate hurry,
Argue and bustle and bargain and worry!
Frenzy yourself into sickness and dizziness —
Christmas is over and Business is Business.

Us Potes

Swift was sweet on Stella;
  Poe had his Lenore;
Burns's fancy turned to Nancy
  And a dozen more.

Pope was quite a trifler;
  Goldsmith was a case;
Byron'd flirt with any skirt
  From Liverpool to Thrace.

Sheridan philandered;
  Shelley, Keats, and Moore
All were there with some affair
  Far from lit'rachoor.

Fickle is the heart of
  Each immortal bard.
Mine alone is made of stone —
  Gotta work too hard.

Footlight Motifs

ANNA HELD

I shall not praise your Gallic ways,
   Nor say that you are sweet;
Nor even tell about the spell
   That brings me to your feet.

I shall devise about your eyes,
   Nor precious words nor choice;
I shall not print a single hint
   In honor of your voice.

I shall not sing of anything
   That makes me genuflect;
Nor grace nor air, nor face nor hair —
   In brief, in no respect.

I shall not praise the heldian ways.
   If you must know, forsooth —
Because that I detest a lie,
   And aim to print the truth.

In Other Words

EMMY WEHLEN

Lady stars from oversea,
    Twinkling in our firmament.
Small the smash you make with me
    Be you ne'er so prominent.
Keener critics may adore you;
Frankly, though, I'm seldom for you.

I was never one who raved
    O'er the pseudo-picturesque
Nor, though young, was I enslaved
    By the art of H. Modjesk.;
And I own I do not care a
Lot about the Perfect Sarah.

Polish ladies leave me cold;
    Dames Italian warm me not;
And, if further truth be told,
    I'm electrified no jot,
Trifle, fragment, ohm, iota,
By th' entire foreign quota.

But, however, still and yet,
    Maugre all my prejudice
I am not so firmly set
    That I will not yield in this:
If I like a lady's way, so
Help me Robert, I will say so!

Footlight Motifs

Fairy, elfin, pixie, sprite,
   Naiad, hamadryad, fay,
Witch and Phantom of Delight
   Such-a-little flow'r-o'-May,
Emmy Wehlen, more than pretty
Subject of this Deathless Ditty!

Wherefore I should like to hint,
   Caring not if it be seen,
Here and now in public print,
   She's considerable queen.
Nothing's left in my thesaurus —
She's a peach, believe me, Mawruss.

EVA TANGUAY

Tell me not, in boastful hollers,
   What her salary may be;
Though it be a million dollars
   It is all the same to me.

Though the universal rumor
   Place her at the top of fun,
To my narrow mind, of humor
   She has absolutely none.

Lives of actresses remind us,
   We can make an awful Hit,
If we only put behind us
   All our Piety and Wit.

In Other Words

Let us then be up and pounding
   Piffle of the kind that flaunts
Its inanity astounding!
   "Give the public what it wants!"

THE CLASSIC DANCE

Isadora, when you dance
   I am bounden by no thrall,
And the Rhythm of old Romance
   Surges o'er me not at all.

Critics with a keener eye,
   Judges with a broader view,
Tell me that your Art is high —
   Wonderful the things you do.

Banal I and low my brow,
   And my bean is built of bone,
For allegiance I vow
   To Montgomery and Stone.

KITTY GORDON

"It is not beauty I demand,
   A crystal brow, the moon's despair,
Nor the snow's daughter, a white hand,
   Nor mermaid's yellow pride of hair."
These lyric lines are not my own;
They're by an elder bard, unknown.

Footlight Motifs

And then he sings of lips and eyes,
   "A bloomy pair of vermeil cheeks,"
Counting her charms in ancient wise,
   As was the custom of the Greeks;
He ends his catalogue, whereat
"They are but gauds," he says — like that.

Which — pardon my discursive style,
   ('Tis thus the British rhymers do;
No vulgar haste to coax the smile.
   [I rather like the plan.   Do you?])
Which, as I started out to say
Before this unforeseen delay —

Which brings me, after false alarms
   And haltings, to this theme of mine:
In brief, to Kitty Gordon's charms
   Gold, ivory and incarnadine.
She is, meseems, a gaudy star
Cold, distant, bright — and there you are.

MARY GARDEN

Mary had a little voice,
   (Unless the crits are wrong),
And everywhere that Mary went
   She took the voice along.

It followed her upon the stage
   (Which isn't far from fact),
It made the audience applaud
   To see Miss Mary act.

In Other Words

They crowded to the opery house;
   They filled each row and tier;
And clapped their hands and split their gloves
   When Mary did appear.

"What makes the folks love Mary so?"
   The eager public cry,
"Why, Mary is the earth's best show!"
   And that's no Barnum lie.

Revised

When the pillow's warm and the sheet is
    torrid,
When you put cold towels on your fervid fore-
    head.
When the breeze won't blow, when the
    moments creep,
When you toss all night and you get no sleep —
    It's hot, by George, it's hot!

The Lost Wheeze

Seated last night at my table
   I was laboring for a laugh
To work into this here colyum,
   In the form of a paragraph.

I know not what I was thinking,
   Or what was within my brain,
But I struck one chord of humor
   That was better than all Mark Twain.

It flooded my littered table
   And my chair of mission oak,
And I said, in my modest manner,
   To myself "That is sure some joke!"

It quieted pain and sorrow
   Like love overcoming strife,
It made me forget the premium
   Due on my well-known life.

It would have made me famous
   All over the East and West,
All people would have pointed
   To the Author of that Great Jest.

In Other Words

I have sought, but I seek it vainly,
    That one Lost Wheeze divine
That one last word in humor,
    That was-to-be-deathless line!

It may be that Death's bright Angel
    Will slip me that joke, I guess,
But that does me no good this morning
    When the page is going to press.

From an Awningless Sanctum

Were it not better done, as others use,
To sport with Amaryllis in the shade?
MILTON.

Dear Amaryllis (you mentioned in "Lycidas"),
  I'm no philanderer, truly I'm not,
But in this office it's sticky and viscid as
  Crab-apple jelly and ten times as hot.

Sternly forbidding, austere, puritanical,
  That is my nature, unardent, severe;
Yet, though the bulk of my verse is mechanical,
  This, Amaryllis, is warmly sincere.

Dear Amaryllis, I hereby import with you:
  'Ryllie, wo wohnst du, proverbial maid?
Tell me, for, oh, I am anxious to sport with
  you,
  If, Amaryllis, you'll furnish the shade,

"On Christmas Day in the Morning"

Dreary the room where dun Despair
Sits unmoved in a broken chair;
Sad is the home where Want, confessed,
Comes to the board a daily guest;
And a woman sits and gazes and weeps
As Innocence in the cradle sleeps.
Bitter and hot are the woman's tears,
And strong with the salt of hopeless years,
And her heart is heavy with Dread and Hate
And she questions Justice whose name is Fate;
And she wonders, too, at the will to live,
As she thinks of the things she cannot give.

And the woman weeps in her selfish woe,
But the grief of another she may not know —
The grief of another she knows not of —
Who hath nowhither to give her love.

From a Paragrapher's Garden of Verses

In winter, when I have to write,
I hate to do my work at night;
In summer, quite the other way,
I hate to have to write by day.

What time the year is at the spring,
I hate to work like anything;
And in the days of early fall
I sort of hate to work at all.

Oh, does it not seem hard to you
That people should have work to do?
But I cannot afford to miss,
And so I pen a pome like this.

Gilbert

Prince of the lambent and elusive smile,
   Dispenser prodigal of light and cheer,
Sweet knight that sable Care dost oft beguile,
   Poet of Truth, take tribute of a tear!

Lines to Margaret, a Singing and Whistling Cook

Woman, attend my warning;
  Hark to mine ultimat;
Done by my hand this morning,
  Done in my five-room flat,
Hark to this warm effusion,
  Ponder on what I write.
This is my firm conclusion,
  Come to but yesternight:

Woman, respect my wishes —
  Can you not cease to sing
While you are washing dishes?
  You are an Awful Thing.
Melody is not in you
  You are from song immune.
Will you not discontinue
  Trying to trail a tune?

Peaceable I and lawful;
  Dreadful of stress and strife;
But — you are worse than awful,
  Spoiling my Joy of Life.
Here is my warning: Cop it.
  Ponder it *con* and *pro*.
Woman, unless you stop it,
  ONE OF US HAS TO GO.

A Pathetic Bit of a Ballad

"You may say for me," said the banker, as he
    sat in his donjon keep,
"That I thank the public for all they've done
    and ——" here he began to weep;
And the sob reporter wrote a yarn that was
    destined to make you cry,
And those who read said, "It's too bad. I'm
    sorry for him, poor guy!"

The sob reporter went to the man as he came
    from the prison cell,
And the man, released, said "On your way!
    I haven't a word to tell."
"But the people," the sob reporter said, "the
    people want to know."
And the man leaned back in his limousine and
    uttered a loud "Ho! Ho!"

Song of the Costofliving

Taking it on percentage with Tennyson.

I come from hunger and from need:
   I make a sudden sally;
I soar with an increasing speed;
   I scamper up an alley.

Up, up I soar in eager flight
   Beyond the wildest rumors,
Until I pass beyond the sight
   Of ultimate consumers.

I chatter, chatter, as I fly,
   Of ice and eggs and leather,
And what makes everything so high —
   The middlemen?   The weather?

Again I soar, and more and more,
   Into the heights I cherish;
And chortle when a hundred score,
   Who cannot see me, perish.

I rise, I soar, I dip, I fly —
   Descend to earth?   Nay, never!
For men may live and men may die,
   But I go up forever.

The Old Man's Discomforts

With obeisances to the estate of R. Southey, dec'd.

"You are cold, Father William," the young
    man cried,
  "You shiver the length of the day;
"You are chill, Father William, your hands
    are as ice,
  Now tell me the reason, I pray."

"In the flat where I live," Father William
    replied,
  "Though it is an expensive demesne.
The heat is turned off from eleven at night
  Till morning at seven-fifteen."

"You are cold, Father William," the young
    man cried
  "Though you live in a beautiful flat,
You constantly swear at the boreal air —
  Pray slip me the reason for that."

"In my costly abode," Father William replied,
  "The casements are fashioned so ill
That the wind enters in till the temp-er-a-ture
  Of my bedroom is way below nil."

The Old Man's Discomforts

"You are cold, Father William," the young
    man cried,
  "As I animadverted before.
And yet you pay many doubloons for your
    rent —
  Pray, Pa, juxtapose me once more."

"The rent that I pay," Father William re-
    plied,
  "Is paid not for windows nor steam;
But the entrance downstairs is of marble and
    gold."
  And that's no impalpable dream.

The Fool

The Fool did on his motley
    And sighed, as who should say:
"If all but me be sobbing,
    Why then must I be gay?

"If all the world be weeping,
    And very life seem wrong,
Why is it mine to fashion
    A whimsy and a song?

"Pray, why must I be merry?"
    — But came no answering word.
For that the world was weeping,
    And none the Fool had heard.

APRIL 19, 1912.

To the Wind: After Gilbert's "To the Terrestrial Globe"

Also after two slumberless nights.

Blow on, thou wind, blow on!
Across, up, down the Drive,
　　　Blow on!
What though I toss till half-past five?
What though I have a charge to keep?
What though I ululate and weep?
What though I cannot get to sleep?
　　Never *you* mind!
　　　　Blow on!

Blow on, thou wind, blow on!
Across my little bed
　　　Blow on!
It's true there's aching in my head;
It's true my room is twenty-two;
My feet are numb; my lips are blue —
But please don't let that worry you!
　　Never *you* mind!
　　　Blow on —
　　　　　　[It blows on.]

To a Lady Complaining of Solitude

[Lines aroused on hearing a song across the area — or
is it aria? — way.]

Lady, I hear your moan,
   Set in a minor key,
Pitched in a plaintive tone,
Triste is your "All alone,
   Nobody here but me."

Lady, I know you not.
   Be you or dark or fair,
Happy or hard your lot,
Who you may be or what,
   Little I know — or care.

But — when you sing that song
   Reeking with woe and ruth —
Lady, to put it strong,
Yours is a statement wrong,
   Far from the well-known truth.

Lady, in brief, you lie.
   Think of me as I rage,
Aiming to versify.
"All alone!"   Am not I,
   Too, in the vicinage?

The Pandean is no Pipe

"Rat-a-tat!" go the rattle-y rivets
   Only a block from this Broadway abode.
Though I were right as a legion of trivets,
   How could I pencil a perishless ode?

"Ting-a-ling-ling!" goes the ring telephonic:
   Haste I to answer it, out in the hall,
"Well?" I intone.   Says the lady, laconic,
   "Hang your receiver up. I didn't call."

Enters a boy who demandeth exchanges;
   Cometh a critic to borrow a match.
Had I the poise of the Appenine ranges,
   Still inspiration would fail to attach.

Day after day do I tease the afflatus,
   Wooing a muse that is too far aloft,
And when I leave, a forlorn literatus,
   Office-mates say, "Gee, that guy's got it
      soft."

"The Poems of Eugene Field"

(Somewhat in the Fieldian manner.)

No gold-reguerdoned poet I to puff a book for
    pelf,
For even I am forced to buy the books I praise
    myself,
Albeit there be those that think that when I
    laud a tome
Its publisher invites me in to make myself at
    home.
Could you but see the monthly bills that stare
    me in the face,
You readily would see that such is not the
    happy case;
Yet once again I toot the horn, again the pen
    I wield
To advertise the Poetry of Eugene Field.

Not Swinburne with his lovely lines that
    lilt their way along,
Not Byron's burning poetry, nor Wordsworth's
    simple song,
Not Kipling's virile balladry, nor Marlowe's
    mighty line,
Not Tennyson's pellucid rhyme, nor Shelley's
    odes divine,

"The Poems of Eugene Field"

Not Dobson's dainty triolets, nor Chaucer's
    sturdy verse;
Not Southey, Calverley nor Hood, nor eke
    Sir Thomas Perc.,
To none of these I bring the bay, to none the
    laurel yield —
My choice is for the Poetry of Eugene Field.

How varied are the poem-themes in which
    that book abounds!
The Apple Pies, the Gosling Stews, the Joys
    Unknown to Lowndes!
And oh, how that dyspeptic apotheosized the
    cooks
And longed for roast-beef very rare, but even
    rarer books!
And wit ye well, how hee ben fain to rede of
    ony knight
Wyth mace and hauberk, helm and glaive,
    and mickle valoure dight;
While in the odes of Q. H. F. his knowledge he
    revealed —
Good sooth, he was a busy bard, was Old
    'Gene Field.

Exalted be the memory of him with whom
    we've smiled,
But blessed thrice the name of him that sang a
    little child.
Let those who will declare the Gentle Poet
    insincere —

In Other Words

I doubt it, like the Carpenter, and check a
    rising tear.
The which is why I celebrate that poet and
    his rhyme
And hint it were a goodly gift to give at
    Christmas time —
Two dollars net, Charles Scribner's Sons —
    Why should it be concealed?
Go, buy that brimming volume by Eugene
    Field!

Success

Success, oh word so ill-defined,
  Oh word that means the same to few!
A myriad meanings all combined
      Are rolled in you.

Is it success to have great wealth
  And all the pleasures it will bring?
Or is it poverty and health,
      As many sing?

Is it success to own estates,
  Vast areas of mines and land,
To have the pow'r to mock the fates;
      Supremely grand;

To have a house with all the things
  That luxury and taste desire;
Treasures to which the richest kings
      May well aspire.

A beautiful and noble wife,
  To have, to hold and to caress —
Is this — are these the things of life
      That make Success?

In Other Words

Has he the great, the true success
   If Love and Fame and Wealth are his —
Is this the way to Happiness?
      You bet it is.

Managerial Tradition

If one should say that Boston girls were pretty
    and athletic —
    As many of them very likely be —
If one should say Chicago maids were cultured
    and esthetic
    And Philadelphia fairies fast and free —

If one depict a Western girl that isn't known
    as "breezy,"
    If one should say a Gotham girl were slow —
It all would be veracious and it should be
    very easy;
But who would ever dare produce the show?

"Christmas Comes but Once a Year"

(As Wordsworth might simply have done it.)

I met a little village child,
 A simple one and poor
As ever crossed the heath at night
 Or went across the moor.

"What do you out so late abroad?"
 I asked that simple child.
She simply looked at me and said,
 The while she simply smiled:

"The seven of us simply live
 A little way from here;
And oh, to-day is Christmas day —
 It comes but once a year."

In many a land and many a clime
 Have I had cause to be,
But never since then have I seen
 Such sweet simplicity.

"Christmas Comes but Once a Year"

(As Austin Dobson might rondeau it, "To a Poet
Bewailing the Paucity of Christmas.")

"Christmas comes but once a year?"
Be it so!   Why interfere?
    Melt but once the silver snows,
    Blossoms only once the rose —
Does it make the rose less dear?

Nay, my silly sonneteer,
Other days may disappear,
    New Year's leaves and May-day goes —
        Christmas comes!

Draws the day of Noël near,
Light the log and mix the cheer!
    Vanish, Care! and perish Prose!
    'Tis the season of rondeaux
Intricately Gallic.   .   .   .   Here
        Christmas comes!

(Being an attempt to parody an eminent young
librettist, author, manager and actor.)

Now, everybody knows that I'm a patriotic
        guy —
            (*By the dawn's early light*)
My birthday and the country's is the 4th day
        of July.
            (*Tramp! Tramp! Tramp! The boys
            are marching.*)

In Other Words

But though I'd like to sing a song about Abe
    Lincoln's birthday,
      (*Just before the battle, mother*)
I think that, on the level, Christmas ought to
    have the first say.

CHORUS

It's a grand old institution,
      (*In Dixie land I'll take my stand*)
  In the Western Hemisphere,
      (*Hail Columbia! Happy land!*)
Then give three cheers for Christmas,
      (*And a tiger*)
  It comes but once a year.

You may have your Decoration Day, your
    New Year's and the rest,
      (*O Columbia! the gem of the ocean!*)
But Christmas Eve on Broadway is the time
    that suits me best.
      (*Maryland! My Maryland!*)
'Tis there you find your dear old pals, the best
    in all the world;
      (*Way down upon the Swanee River!*)
'Tis there you find the best of all the fellows
    and the girls.

CHORUS

It's a grand old institution, etc.

106

"Christmas Comes but Once a Year"

(Somewhat in the Kipling manner.)

*Now these are the things that Christmas brings,
     the things of the tide of Yule,
And this is the way of that dreadsome day, as it
     goes by the swerveless rule:*

Days and weeks the lady seeks to purchase of a
     trinket,
  (Shop! shop! shop!   O the terror of the
  trade!)
Buyin' of a gift o' love?   Well, ye better think
     it —
  Aimin' at the sergeant who is passin' on
  parade.
        And it's shop, shop, shop!
        Till the sweat begins to drop!
  Never was a present yet worth a charge o'
  hop.

Sergeant Burr has bought for her a bally
     di'mond jewel
  (Shop! shop! shop!   O the terror of the
  trade!)
Never met a orfcer yet as wasn't cold an' cruel
  (O the wily sergeant, and ah, the willing
  maid!)
        And it's shop! shop! shop!
        Till the sweat begins to drop —
  Never was a present yet worth a charge o'
  hop!

In Other Words

Now those are the things that Christmas brings,
the things of the tide of Yule,
And that is the way of that dreadsome day, as it
goes by the swerveless rule!

(In Hood's worst manner.)

JOCOSE JOE STENCIL

A Bathetic Ballad

Joe Stencil was a nice young man,
   And eke a shipping clerk,
Although he'd often work to love,
   He never loved to work.

One day he met with Minnie Brown,
   And fain would be her lover,
But Minnie overlooked him quite,
   Although he looked her over.

"O Minnie Brown! O Minnie Brown!
   Why think you not of me?"
"The more I think of you," she said,
   "The less I think," said she.

"O Minnie Brown! O Minnie Brown!
   I think it would be proper,
Although I but a shipper am,
   If I should be a shopper.

"Christmas Comes but Once a Year"

"Be not so adamant," said Joe,
    "I aim not to deceive.
I'll be your Christmas Adam, if
    You'll be my Christmas Eve."

Joe Stencil then began to sing
    Of all the joy he'd bring her:
"Ah, Minnie, when I sing to you,
    I am a minnesinger."

"O Joseph, cut the comedy,
    You've had an overdose;
Although I like to hear you, Joe
    I like you less jocose."

"O Min, I know the jokes are not
    Particularly good,
But they are as jest as good as some
    You'll find in Thomas Hood.

"Only upon the Christmas day
    Shall I my puns rehearse,
For though they are quite prosy, yet
    You know they might be verse."

And so 'tis but a single day
    This double pair most fear,
And they rejoice that Christmas day
    Comes only once a year.

In Other Words

(As Lord Byron might sing it, in a minor.)

Farewell! And if within that breast
    Affection's spark shall smolder still,
Fan it to flame and quench the rest,
    And let the world say what it will.

Farewell! Farewell! O wintry word
    That chills and numbs this aching heart —
This heart that hath so often erred,
    But softens when 'tis time to part.

Farewell! Farewell! Farewell! And though
    This heart shall be an empty thing,
Thou canst not fathom half the woe
    That lies within it when I sing.

Farewell! Farewell! Farewell! Oh, dear,
    Of all that dearest is to me,
Though Christmas comes but once a year,
    My farewells come more frequently.

(Being an attempt to get away with Thomas Moore's
manner.)

Oh, sweet is the scent of the rose in the morn-
    ing,
    And fresh is the flower besprinkled with dew,
But sweeter and fresher thy face is, mavour-
    neen,
    As pure as the lily and whiter of hue.

"Christmas Comes but Once a Year"

Oh, silk was the shawl that I last saw her
    wearing,
    And sad are the moorlands and sad are the
      leas.
And sadder the songs that they sing about
    Erin,
    And saddest the way that they drop off the
      g's.

Oh, red is the berry that grows on the holly,
    And tender the mem'ry of vanished things
      dear,
And this is the thought of my sweet melan-
    choly,
    That Christmas comes once and but once in
      the year.

(In one of Frank L. Stanton's manners.)

I

Chris'mus am a-comin',
    Cahve de possum meat!
My! dem sweet potatoes
    Am mighty good to eat.

II

Chris'mus am a-comin',
    Down in Geo'gy lan';
Chris'mus am a-comin',
    Don' yo un'er'stan'?

In Other Words

III

Chris'mus am a-comin',
Hear, believers, hear,
Chris'mus come to Geo'gy
Only wunst a year.

(Stanzas **IV** to **CLI** supplied on demand.)

(As Martin Farquhar Tupper might have obscured it.)

Now this is an indisputable fact,
   And that is one which no one can dispute;
As true as that a diplomat needs tact,
   As true as that an apple is a fruit,
None can deny what I have said; What I
Have said, I say, nobody can deny.

And if none can gainsay what I have said,
   Then that which I have said none can gain-
     say,
A man who's passed away is known as dead;
   Dead is a person who has passed away.
But this is not what I began to sing;
What I began to say is not this thing.

Now this is what I hold as solemn truth,
   And solemn truth is that which is not gay.
A man of sixty years is not a youth,
   Nor are black tresses those completely gray.
But this is clear as glass, as glass is clear:
The day of Christmas comes but once a year.

112

"Christmas Comes but Once a Year"

(As Swinburne might treat it.)

As a day that dawns when the dark is dimmer,
   Sodden and sad as a sunless sea,
Gray and green as a glaring glimmer,
   Burnished and bright in its gilded glee.
Gone the guerdon and gone the glories,
   Dead or ever the day was born —
Dead as a devilish dove, Dolores,
   Mother of misery, made to mourn!

Thou hast bared thy breast to the boreal
     breezes
   Sibilant, stark, as the soul of sin,
Chill and cheap as a Cheshire cheese is,
   Gloriously glad as an elinorglyn!
Winds that whimper and winds that whistle
   Faster far than the phantom of fear.
O Dolores, the toe of mistle!
   Christmas comes! and but once a year.

After Samuel Rogers

Go! you may call it madness, folly;
  You shall not chase my gloom away.
There's such a charm in melancholy
  I would not, if I could, be gay.

For me the month is never May.
  Fate hurls at me a daily volley.
The nights are black, the noons are gray —
  Go! you may call it madness, folly.

Go, frivolers, to your fi-nale!
  Go, butterflies, go on and play!
You make no hit with me.   By golly,
  You shall not chase my gloom away!

Alas! the heavy price we pay
  For Life her mistletoe and holly!
The shadow's longer than the ray.
  There's such a charm in melancholy!

Each time I meet another dollie
  She takes a look and says: "Nay, nay!"
And while I'm beating for the trolley
  I would not, if I could, be gay.

114

After Samuel Rogers

How simple is the metric jolly!
  Though meaningless as shredded hay,
Though very rare the rhymes in olly,
  How smooth these rondeaux redoublées
                       Go!

The Diplomaniacs

"The Puritans and Liberty";
  "The Power of the Press";
"The Portuguese in History";
  And "What Is True Success?"

"The Elements of National Wealth";
  "The Fixedness of Mars";
"Is Money Greater than Good Health?"
  And "Night Brings Out the Stars."

"The Greatness of Obedience";
  "The Mission of Research";
"Will Hegel's Fame Have Permanence?"
  "Which Greater — State or Church?"

"*Audaces Fortuna Juvat*";
  "America and Spain";
"*Hoc Opus Finis Coronat,*"
  "Psychology of Pain."

"The Joy that Education brings";
  "Antonian Triremes" —
Are but a few of many things
  For graduation themes.

Rondel

Bribery, suicide, crime —
  Ain't it a deuce of a note
Trying to fashion a rhyme —
  One that exchanges will quote?
  Why do the papers devote
Pages and pages to grime,
Bribery, suicide, crime?
  Ain't it a deuce of a note?

  Once when the psalter I smote
Sounds that were sweet and sublime
  Came; but to-day if a pote
Echoes the theme of his time —
Bribery, Suicide, Crime —
  Ain't it a deuce of a note?

To the Waltonian Bards

(Aroused by the fact that fourteen of our exchanges this morning contain "Fishin'" poems.)

Poets that prate of the worry of working
  During the days of a sultry July,
Prate of the pleasure undoubtedly lurking,
  Lurking, we say, in the rod and the fly —

Bards who descant on the wonders of fishing,
  Angling for pickerel, "muskie" and trout,
Voicing that awful, inevitable "wishing" —
  Can it, forget it, let go, cut it out.

Joys piscatorial may be delightful,
  Singing them, though, is a bit of a pest;
Ours not the wish to be acid or spiteful,
  But, brother bards, won't you give us a rest?

Triolettuce Salad

Ingredients by Goldsmith, Mallet, Trowbridge and Coleridge.   Stirred by us with a fountain pen this day.

Good people all, of every sort,
  Give ear unto my song.
Or slim or stout, or tall or short,
Good people all, of every sort,
Attend ye to my metric sport
  Until I sound the gong.
Good people all, of every sort,
  Give ear unto my song.

'Twas at the silent, solemn hour
  When night and morning meet.
Within my cozy five-room bow'r,
T'was at the silent solemn hour,
When Bill, in tones of dreadful pow'r,
  Yelled: "HEY, GIDDAP THERE, PETE!"
'Twas at the silent, solemn hour
  When night and morning meet!

119

In Other Words

The night was made for cooling shade,
  For silence and for sleep.
O mighty line by Trowbridge made —
"The night was made for cooling shade"
I hear the garbage-can brigade,
  And murmur, cursing deep:
"The night was made for cooling shade,
  For silence and for sleep."

Oh, sleep! it is a gentle thing,
  Beloved from pole to pole!
Ah, Coleridge, thou who daredst to sing
"Oh, sleep! it is a gentle thing!"
Thou never heardst the ash can's bing,
  Else blank had been that scroll:
Oh, sleep! it is a gentle thing
  Beloved from pole to pole!

The Easy Giggle

Showing how the leading comedian may always get
a certain hand.

When the vein of comicality
Is voided of vitality,
   And all the silly little
   Tattle-tittle
       Has been done,
There always is a visible
Assurance of the risible
   By dexterously using
   An amusing
       Little pun.

CHORUS

You can always get a laugh with that.
Or by joshing any lady who is fat,
   When you sing the second stanza,
   Speak of Dressler or Friganza —
You can always get a line with that,

In Other Words

The ways of being humorous
Are not so very numerous;
  They'll laugh until they're crying
  When you're guying
    New Rochelle;
And nearly all humanity
Will giggle at profanity —
  The whole entire gamut
  Clear from " ⸺ ⸺ "
    Down to " ⸺. "

CHORUS
You can always get a laugh with that —
Never try to hit the crowd above the hat,
  If you want to get 'em shrieking,
  Imitate a lady speaking —
You can always get a laugh with that.

DANCE

The Ballade of the Northern Girl

Her manner was perfectly sweet
   And golden the hue of her hair;
She was pretty, of course, and petite;
   And when you would ask of her: "Where
   Are you from?" she would answer: "Eau
      Claire,
Wisconsin. What? 'Baltimore'? Nixie!
   What made you think I was from
      there?" . . . .
   She always applauded at "Dixie."

She was fair from her head to her feet;
   She was — oh, description's despair,
As she rose from her orchestra seat
   And pounded her gloves to a tear —
   This dear little maid from Bellaire,
Ohio. Ingenuous, tricksy.
   "New Orleans? No! . . . How you
      stare!" . . . .
She always applauded at "Dixie."

In Other Words

She is found in the shop and the street;
   She sits in a restaurant chair;
She may be *bourgeois* or *élite;*
   But she thrills to the Southerner's air.
   From Portsmouth, N. H., and Big Bear,
N. Y., this ubiquitous pixie.
   Though blue was her grandfather's wear,
She always applauded at "Dixie."

L'ENVOI

O Epitaph-makers, prepare
   This sentence, and chisel it quick, see:
HERE LIETH MISS LEGION, THE FAIR:
SHE ALWAYS APPLAUDED AT "DIXIE."

Lines on the Sabbath

To a person loving leisure in a high and heap-
    ing measure
  What a joyaunce, what a treasure is a Sun-
    day afternoon!
Of diversions there are plenty, from the *dolce
far niente*
  Joys to seventeen or twenty things to kill a
    day in June.

One may journey in a motor, go to Coney in a
    boat, or
  Pass the rickey down the throat, or mix the
    julep with the mint;
Do you love it cool and pretty, there are Deal,
    Atlantic City,
  And some others that my ditty hasn't room
    enough to print.

For the Phyllises there's wooing while the
    Corydons are suing;
  There is walking and canoeing, there are
    hammocks, there are swings;
And for those that have the notion there's the
    broad Atlantic Ocean
  For a dip — and Land o' Goshen! — there's
    a myriad of things!

In Other Words

One may read a little when it strikes one's
    fancy — Arnold Bennett,
  H. G. Wells, or what the Senate has to say
    on this or that —
But of all the things delighting and alluring
    and exciting,
  Truly, none of them is writing in a stuffy
    Harlem flat.

"The Landing of the Pilgrim Fathers"

(The Pilgrim Fathers have virtues ascribed to them
which they never possessed—Prof. ALBERT BUSHNELL
HART.)

The breaking waves dashed high
   On a warm and pleasant coast,
And the woods against an azure sky
   Their Parrish branches toss'd;

And the summer night hung dark
   The hills and waters o'er,
When those summer tourists moor'd their
     bark
   On the swell New England shore.

Not as the conqueror comes,
   They, the weak-hearted, came.
But, like a bunch of exiled bums,
   Trying to beat the game.

There were men with thinning hair
   Amidst that pilgrim class;
Why had they come to wither there
   In a burg like Plymouth, Mass.?

In Other Words

What did they there for weeks?
  I do not know, I'm sure,
Unless, perhaps, they made   "Antiques"
  And "real old furniture."

The Exile of Erin

(Mr. Thomas Campbell's heirs are apologized to.)

There came to the flat a poor exile of Erin,
    Her brogue was as thick as a shamrock
        purée,
The calico dress that our Maggie was wearin'
    Was ragged as army flags all shot away;
She was timid and meek, she would stand
        without hitchin';
She labored all day in the hot little kitchen;
She washed and she ironed and hummed most
        bewitchin',
    The beautiful anthem of Erin go bragh.

All friendless and lonely was Maggie O'Ryan,
    No sweethearts there came her lone heart to
        beguile;
Yet cheerful and gladsome, nor sobbin' nor
        sighin',
    For friends that were left in the Emerald
        Isle;
No threnody hers for the land she was born in;
She always arose before six in the mornin',
And sang the sweet strains of her "Erin
        Mavourneen" —
    The minor melodics of Erin go bragh.

In Other Words

Alas, as the poet declares, Tempus fidgets!
    'Tis only a month since she came to our
      shore.
But since she's met Norahs and Katies and
      Bridgets,
    Ochone! our acushla is happy no more!
She started to work for a weekly three-fifty;
But now she gets seven, her habits are thrifty.
Her dress it is faultless and stylishly nifty —
    And Tuesdays and Thursdays and Satur-
      days out.

Of Course You Would

If you had to make some verses on the topics
of the day,
    You would read the morning papers rather
fully;
For you'd like to find a theme to make your
readers shout: "Hooray!"
    And to make your Dear Employer say:
"That's bully!"

You would scan aforesaid journals with a very
fine-tooth comb
    (With the metaphors I'm something of a
mixer.)
For a nifty little subject you could pad into a
pome;
    And you'd have to be about it pretty quick,
sir.

You would read the Morse indictment; you
would read of plot and crime;
    You might read about a meeting suffragetty;
But you'd say: "Them ain't no matters for to
put in classic rhyme,"
    And no more would be the Central loans and
Hetty.

In Other Words

You would read how Mr. Vanderbilt and
    others had been robbed;
  You would read or skip some speeches at a
    dinner;
You would see a Gothic headline saying:
    "Pretty Woman Mobbed,"
  And you'd read a few critiques of Otis
    Skinner.

You would read about the blow-up in the tun-
    nel yesternoon;
  You would read — oh, yes you would — the
    ice inquiry;
You would read about the chap who lived a
    week in a balloon,
  And you'd find that every theme was
    uninspiry.

Oh, you'd worry like the mischief on your
    foolish daily pome,
  For you'd want to do it prettily and nicely,
And after doing all of this you'd hit the breeze
    for home.
    *   *   *   *

  And that's the way that I should do, pre-
    cisely.

True Comfort

(There is nothing quite so comforting in this life as a word of five syllables. — MR. W. PETT RIDGE.)

Brevity! Heavens, what inefficaciousness!
  Brevity! Piffle! A mere fabulosity!
Comfort is only a great ostentatiousness;
  Quiet is only in vociferosity.

Shortness in writing denotes adolescency,
  Me for an erudite, big etymologist —
One who can tell you the true delitescency
  Found in the brain of a phytopathologist.

Still, I believe that a man pharmaceutical
  Seems, in a measure, to be reimbursable,
Arguing thus, it seems quite therapeutical
  Voters for Taft are to be incoercible.

Which, to a mind beyond doubt algebraical,
  Seems but the rankest of rank meretricious-
     ness,
Silly and sad, not to say pharisaical;
  Bless you! the thing is but old superstitious-
     ness!

In Other Words

Ah!   How I flounder in mad inconclusiveness!
  Mad is this quinquepedalian verbosity.
"Comfort?"   Great heavings!   What   mad
    perdiffusiveness —
  Look at me here in complete comatosity!

To Gelett Burgess

I never saw a Sulphite.   No,
  I never hope to see one;
I am acquiring brain fag, though,
  Endeavoring to be one.

Bacchanalian Songs

(The *American Magazine* advances that most of the
drinking songs are pretty poor stuff.)

These endless aimless, footless airs!
   Carousers start and never end 'em:
"We're Here Because"; "Nobody Cares";
       "Nunc Est Bibendum."

'Tis true.   The lyric of the souse
   Is often far from a divine song,
Be it "Another on the House"
       Or Hovey's "Stein Song."

A myriad more the drinking cuss
   Will carol as the hours grow slender?
"Lang Soll Er Leben" and "Give Us
       A Drink, Bartender!"

Poor stuff, in sooth.   Yet though the loads
   May warble dithyrambics wishy,
Meseems I know no stirring odes
       To Milk-and-Vichy.

On a Certain Propensity of Bootblacks to Toy with the Shoelaces of the Shinee

Polishing little rapscallion,
   Shining away at my shoes,
Be thou or Greek or Italian,
   Thou art the one I accuse;
Ruin my tans with thy tarnish,
   That were a crime to condone,
But, when thou smearest the varnish,
   Leave thou my laces alone!

Utterly spoil and demolish
   All of the calfskin I wear,
Wreak, with thy poisonous polish,
   Ruin — 'tis little I care.
But, as thou needest thy nickel,
   Listen to me as I moan:
"Cease thou mine ankles to tickle!
   Leave thou my laces alone!"

Fiend, how thou watchest me wriggle!
   Ghoul, how thou watchest me wince!
Whiles that thou hidest a giggle
   Under thy Genoan squints.
Hark!　I shall — be this a warning
   Final and straight from my throne!
Kick in thy features some morning,
   An thou leav'st not my laces alone!

Christmas Cards

Being the songs of an old Scrooge

I.   TO A JANITOR

Native of Sweden or Norway,
   Tyrant of terrible type,
Standing around in the doorway,
   Smoking a miserable pipe —

Thou who refusest to steam up,
   Thou who denyest me heat,
Thou who wilt not send my cream up,
   Thou who purloinest my meat —

Father of infants whose weeping
   All through the perilous night
Loudly inhibits my sleeping —
   Read, if thou canst, what I write:

Why, at this holiday season,
   Should I drop into the slot
Money?   There isn't a reason;
   Therefore, old chap, I shall not.

In Other Words

II. TO A STENOGRAPHER

Person feminine of gender,
  Pounding at the lettered keys,
Think you that I should surrender
Tribute, be it ne'er so slender?
  Lithe and listen, please:

You who, chafing at your fetters,
  Say you "Do not have to work,"
Queen of pompadoured coquetters
How you hate to take my letters!
  How you love to shirk!

You who take two hours for luncheon —
  Cake and soda, as it seems,
Being all that make your nuncheon,
While all afternoon you munch on
  Callow chocolate creams.

Typist, it is truth I'm telling —
  Pardon mine insurgency —
But, O maid at work rebelling,
Scorner of the rules of spelling,
  Not a cent from me!

Christmas Cards

III.   TO AN ELEVATOR BOY

You leave me waiting on my floor,
   Although I press the button hard.
Day after day do you ignore
      This bard.

I walk downstairs; a tiresome task
   For one aweary, worn and old.
And now at Christmas-time you ask
      For gold!

Shall I a good cigar deny
   Myself?   A quarter?   Make your lot
A bit more bearable?   Well, I
      Guess not!

IV.   TO A COOK

Foreign genius culinary,
   Proud but inefficient cook,
Gretchen, Olga, Hulda, Mary,
      Look:

Haply thou expect'st a present
   As the smallest of thy dues,
Hearken!   Thou shalt hear unpleasant
      News.

In Other Words

Hast thou ever tried to study
    What my palate might allure?
Dost thou make the coffee muddy?
        Sure.

Though I like a peeled tomato,
    Do I get it thataway?
Do I get a baked potato?
        Nay.

Though I like my steak the rarest,
    Red as the Milwaukee bricks,
Thy results but prove thou carest
        Nix.

Therefore let this be the burden
    Of this bit of deathless dope:
Dost thou get a Christmas guerdon?
        Nope!

Thanking One and All.

[If it were generally known how many writers who have achieved success have practically been made by editors endowed with the gift of helping the young author to find himself, the public would be indeed surprised. Once in a while one may be startled by some grateful communication or dedication expressive of such literary indebtedness, but this is rare. It must be owned that the attitude of the successful author is usually one of self-congratulation. — *Boston Herald*.

Of me, good sooth, none ever wrote
   "How sharper than a serpent's tooth
It is to have a thankless pote!"
   For wit ye well, this Tower of Truth
Had never seen the l. of d.
   Unless the costly linotyper
Had set my stuff, that it might be
   Emblazoned in this evening pyper.

And if the make-up should refuse
   To place my gems as I request,
Where then would be the motley muse?
   Where then my japery and jest?
And if the paper mill shut down
   Or leaden type no more were minted,
Where then would be my fair renown?
   Where I, with priceless pomes unprinted?

In Other Words

So say not that the trait is rare;
   Us authors is a grateful crew.
Our aim is ever to be fair,
   And give the angel all his due:
Brown's grammar, Noah Webster's tome
   And Walker on Versification
All help me when I pull a pome —
   My stuff is all collaboration.

"Ungrateful?" Nay! My lightest line
   Is due to others more than me.
No paragraph is wholly mine;
   No verse I own in simple fee.
If even the cashier himself,
   Some Saturday when I endeavor
To grab my gold, refused me pelf,
   I'd give up Litrachoor forever.

Lines in Appreciation of a Lady's Art

Madura maid that o'er the stove holdeth
    despotic sway,
Small is the labor that you do, though great
    your weekly pay,
Far from a Savarin are you in the rôle that you
    have picked,
Tortoni could have beaten you from clams to
    Benedict.
Nay, I'll make one exception, and one that
    bids me sing
Your o. f. strob'ry shortcake, a Rare and
    Perfect Thing.

In many a line of cooking your ineptitude is
    great,
You have three afternoons a week, you come
    each morning late.
You burn an awful lot of gas, you waste a lot
    of stuff,
Your soups are generally weak, your steaks
    are always tough,
Yet here is to Virginia, the state that gave you
    birth,
And your o. f. strob'ry short cake, the Finest
    Thing on Earth!

In Other Words

Madura maiden, rob a bank, yet should you
    be enthroned,
Commit a century of crime, yet shall you be
    condoned
So long as you may build those joys, those
    Benisons of Bliss,
Whose memory is with me now as I unlimber
    this;
Whose recollection this here apostrophic stuff
    has stirred
On your o. f. strob'ry shortcake, which is
    Cooking's Final Word.

For Commuters Only

PLAIN APPEARS THE PRINTED WORD
    IN THE LIGHT OF DAY;
NOT A LETTER OF IT BLURRED—
    IT APPEARS THIS WAY.
Goin gthr oughtatun nelth ough;
    Lett ersf lyandflit;
Sylla blesa re wab bly — so —
    Evernoticeit?

Inept Quotation's Artificial Aid

It was a friar of orders gray,
   And he stoppeth one of three:
I chanced to see at break of day
   That not impossible She.

"I was with Grant — " the stranger said —
   By the nine gods he swore —
For here, forlorn and lost I tread
   Beside a human door.

Stay, lady, stay for mercy's sake!
   How glazed each weary eye!
And could I ever keep awake
   Till a' the seas gang dry?

Love still hath something of the sea,
   In the first sweet sleep of night;
Whate'er the years may bring to me,
   Fond mem'ry brings the light.

I hear a voice you cannot hear,
   Beside the Springs of Dove;
And she is grown so dear, so dear,
   She never told her love.

In Other Words

In Xanadu did Kubla Khan
    Look backward with a smile.
The apparel oft proclaims the man,
    And only man is vile.

I have set my life upon a cast —
    To die were far more sweet —
As through on Alpine village passed
    The print of Lucy's feet.

Drink to me only with thine eyes
    To drive dull care away.
In Venice on the Bridge on Sighs,
    Upon a truss of hay.

I never saw a purple cow
    Or nursed a dear gazelle;
When pain and anguish wring the brow
    I only feel Farewell!

She left us in the bloom of May,
    When night and morning meet,
Yet some maintain that to this day
    Her voice is low and sweet.

If this fair rose offend thy sight
    In faëry lands forlorn,
She was a Phantom of Delight
    Breast high amid the corn.

146

Inept Quotation's Artificial Aid

For what avail the plough or sail?
  Men were deceivers ever.
Turn, gentle hermit of the dale,
  And let who will be clever.

I prithee send me back my heart,
  Half hidden from the eye;
'Tis of man's life a thing apart —
  Good-bye, my lover, good-bye!

Some Speeches

Now glory to our holy cause, from whence all
    glories spring,
And glory to our candidate, who stands for
    everything.
So, gentlemen, I nominate that leader of the
    cause,
That noble man, that swerveless head, Wis-
    consin's [*Great applause*].

From where the pine-clad hills of Maine in
    fronded beauty stand,
To where the jagged Rockies reach across this
    lovely land,
Is heard the name that echoes over valley and
    through chasm,
The name of — need I mention it — of [*Great
    enthusiasm*].

Ah, gentlemen assembled in this gre-eat con-
    vention hall,
This land of ours is fairest on the whole
    terrestrial ball;
And who so fit, from Boston to where rolls the
    Oregon,
To steer the Ship of State as [*Cries of "Louder!"
    and "Go on!"*]

148

Some Speeches

That brave, intrepid, fearless, dauntless, wise,
    courageous one,
That plain and honest Democrat, Rhode
    Island's favorite son,
Who loathes the predatory rich, the wicked
    trust and grafter,
That sterling statesman, need I say [*Continued
    cheers and laughter*].

Ohio offers up a name requiring no laudation
To gain for him the honor of this glorious
    nomination;
The choice of all this big broad land is he, to all
    appearing
I bring the name of William Howard [*Loud
    and mighty cheering*].

But who has put the nation where it proudly
    stands to-day?
What is the greatest, biggest name in all these
    U. S. A.?
The name of Theo [*Reader, this applause you'll
    have to guess,
For truly, there be limits to the power of the press*].

NO TROUBLE TO SHOW GOODS

[For the benefit of advertisers, present and prospective, it should be stated that these are only a few of the publisher's kinds of type.]

Speak gently to the printer man,
 His work is pretty hard;
Besides, he does the best he can
 To help along a bard.

O ever ready his response
 To anything we ask,
Though we demand a hundred font
 He would not curse his task.

And yet his lot is not a pipe;
 Small wonder he is vexed,
If we mark this for Jensen type,
 𝔄𝔫𝔡 𝔱𝔥𝔦𝔰 𝔣𝔬𝔯 ℭ𝔞𝔰𝔩𝔬𝔫 𝔗𝔢𝔵𝔱.

No Trouble to Show Goods

Run this, we pray, in Elzevir;
   This in Devinne Slope;
Put this in Gothic, plain and clear;
   In Blanchard set this dope.

Let this line in Long Primer stand,
   And this in Century Bold style;
This in 8-point John Alden, and
   This 10-point Cheltenham Old Style.

In Modern Roman set this here;
   𝕿𝖍𝖎𝖘 𝕿𝖎𝖋𝖋𝖆𝖓𝖞 𝕿𝖊𝖝𝖙, 𝖕𝖊𝖗𝖍𝖆𝖕𝖘;
This goes in regular brevier,
   AND THIS IN AGATE CAPS.

So do not scorn the printer man
   Whose labor is so tough—
He does the very best he can
   To help us with our stuff.

THE END

THE COUNTRY LIFE PRESS
GARDEN CITY, N. Y.